PIONUS PARROT

Every detailed information you need to know about the pionus parrot. Their behaviors, feeding and reasons while they make amazing pet

CALLAN BASIL

Table of Contents

CHAPTER ONE

INTRODUCTION

Pionus parrots are seemed as super pets, even though some species are very rare in captivity. Maximum normally kept species are the Blue-headed, Maximillian (Scaly-headed) and White-Capped.

Others, such as the Dusky and the Bronze-winged have end up more common because of captive breeding.

CHAPTER TWO

BEHAVIOR AND CONDUCT OF PIONUS PARROT

Pionus parrots aren't recognized to be cuddly birds and can be described as reserved. Once they may be bonded, but, they prefer to be preened (their heads and necks scratched). They may be not especially playful, and do now not revel in being wrestled with or flipped on their backs, however they do provide noninvasive companionship and are fascinating partner animals.

Whilst excited or nervous, birds of this genus can also make a feature wheezing or snorting sound this is sometimes wrong for a sign of misery. Others freeze while scared. They also have a musky or sweet scent that some humans discover unpleasant, but others experience.

They are not the best talkers -- in reality some pionuses can also by no means analyze to speak. The clarity of Pionus "speech" levels from instead clear to words handiest a mother may want to recognize. This varies greatly with individuals. Most Pionus do love to examine new and interesting sounds.

CHAPTER THREE

REASONS WHY PIONUS PARROT MAKES GOOD PET

Pionus parrots are acknowledged for his or her quiet (compared to many different parrots) and reserved natures. not like some other associate parrots, aviculturists have mentioned that they are not specially energetic, and do no longer typically experience palms-on play (as an example, being flipped on their backs), but they do offer companionship and are described as gentle and charming pets.

The Pionus parrots are devoted to their proprietors and thrive on attention - however, some of them, especially men, might also bond with one character and aggressively shield that man or woman from perceived risks, including different family individuals. They're lively by way of nature and may come to be obese if carefully constrained.

Even though those parrots are less noisy birds than other parrots, they do make mild, excessive-pitched squeaking calls that might annoy people who are touchy to noise.

While excited or worried, birds of this genus emit a function wheezing or snorting sound this is every now and then flawed for a sign of misery, or a symptom of sickness. They also supply off a musky or candy smell that a few caretakers discover unsightly, but others experience.

Pionus parrots are prone to obesity, nutrition A deficiency, and aspergillosis in captivity.

• Nutrition A promotes appetite, digestion, and

additionally increases resistance to infection and to a few parasites

Biting: The pionus parrots aren't known to be biters; however they can damage your pores and skin if they're scared or startled; or really do not need to be treated for a few purposes (perhaps no longer bonded). The skilled parrot owner might be capable of study their parrot's body language to realize when he or she does now not need to be handled. This all being said, their bites are generally now not nearly as fierce because the bites of different birds and, consequently, they do make a terrific choice for all people who's

intimidated with the aid of parrot
beaks.

CHAPTER FOUR

HOW TO TRAIN YOUR PIONUS PARROT

Interest: The Pionus parrots call for much less time than their large cousins. As long as they're given enough attention by means of their owner inside the morning and/or night (at the least a couple of hours), they normally may be left alone during the day. They must accept the possibility to exercising outdoor the cage and enjoy sports with their proprietor. Birds that spend most of the day within the cage also must be given a huge cage that will accommodate toys and room for exercising. Environmental upgrades, which include leaving the TV or radio on for amusement, are also advocated.

Longevity:

You and your pet bird stay a median of 25 years. Pionus can stay to be over 40 and regularly they stay handiest 3 or 10 years because of accidents and negative nutrition.

Persona:

Pionus parrots are commonly gentle and loving in nature and

make devoted circle of relatives pets. They share the sweet and fun disposition in their associated cousins. They are normally easy-going and wise. Those non-public traits make them suitable applicants for first-time hen owners. Those birds are also top notch alternatives for apartment dwellers, because of their smooth maintenance and calm character.

Pet proprietors usually describe them as inquisitive and sociable parrots that may without problems be tamed. They are less apart to chew than other parrots.

Despite the fact that they may not known for their speaking competencies, with a touch bit of education, some can also learn to mimic (although not all examine to talk!).

They revel in frequent baths as this allows keeping their plumage in accurate condition.

Despite the fact that a medium-sized parrot cage is appropriate for a pionus, large size cages will permit them to move approximately greater freely and provide greater space for toys. These playful birds do need toys to maintain them entertained. They appear to be mainly fond of swings.

The Pionus parrots thrive on attention - however, some of them, in particular adult males, can also bond with one individual and aggressively protect that man or woman from perceived dangers, inclusive of other family participants.

Those birds are lively by using nature and can become obese if carefully confined. Despite the fact that those parrots are much less noisy birds than other parrots, they do make mild, excessive-pitched squeaking calls that could worsen folks that are touchy to noise.

Caring for your Pionus:

The Pionus is a totally lively parrot and wishes the biggest space that your private home can accommodate - preferably, this parrot should be capable of fly from perch to perch, specifically so if the pionus is stored in the cage maximum of the day. This being said, however roomy the cage, every bird should be allowed to be out of the cage for not less than 3 hours every day. Many birds can spend a good deal in their time on a play pen or parrot perch. As they are now not robust chewers, durable cage production isn't always as vital as it would be for the biggest species of parrots. They may be technically willing and learn how to open locks pretty quick and locks or get away-proof latches may be encouraged.

CHAPTER FIVE

FEEDING YOUR PIONUS PARROT

Most pet store proprietors and Pionus parrot fanciers who run web sites will tell you that it is vital that your bird is fed a business pellet feed. I'm no fan of processed food, and a Pionus or every other parrot will do simply as well if you feed him clearly. After sharing my granola in the morning, my Pionus receives a slice of papaya or different clean fruit, a banana, and a few tablespoons of ardor fruit on pinnacle of his Lovebird seed mix.

Later in the morning, he will get a tiny slice of cheese, possibly a bit of hen, uncooked vegetables (carrots and squash on a string), and on a few days, a tiny chew of scrambled eggs. After lunch, I can damage open a clean coconut for him and the opposite birds.

Is so much fresh fruit herbal? Sure, it's far, and it is the manner that Pionus parrots continue to exist inside the wild. The entire culmination you provide need to be freed from pesticides. Your pionus parrot is small and could not capable of resist the buildup of pollutants over his lengthy lifestyles.

Parrots do now not want to be fed a commercial food regimen. The "100% whole" pellets that you purchase are cooked to extend shelf lifestyles, and most of the nutrients are destroyed by way of that cooking procedure. Parrots do, however, want get admission to all varieties of sparkling meals. All of the nutrients he desires can be furnished naturally.

CHAPTER SIX

CHARACTERISTICS OF PIONUS PARROT

All parrots are beautiful, however in my view, Pionus parrots are some of the first-class searching birds round, regardless of what some other parrot owners will declare. The many species of Macaw are without a doubt extra flashy, but the Pionus's colorings are superb. I have the blue-headed range, which I assume is the maximum attractive, but there are numerous others to be had in the pet change.

Pionus birds aren't too huge, status handiest approximately 25 cm and weighing handiest about 250 grams. He is a great deal too large for a parakeet cage but small sufficient to slip between the bars of a cage made for an Amazon or Macaw. If you are nonetheless searching, buy the most important enclosure you can manage to pay for and test on cages used to house a breeding pair of Cockatiels.

And make certain you constantly have plenty of area. They stay approximately 40 years; however loads of Pionus are recognized to be around even longer. If you do decide to deliver a fowl home, remember that this is a long-time period dedication. If bought for a younger individual, they may do okay if some other fowl is delivered later, however the new owner wishes to provide all of his birds a few attention and free time far from the cage.

While taking your bird out to socialize, you could train your Pionus numerous hints however may not be capable of train him to speak. Some humans discover this very crucial.

Inside the wild, Pionus breed in useless coconut bushes, high and out of the reach of different animals. In the domestic, they are bred however they're not as clean as a few other parrot species, which might be one of the motives that they're a luxurious puppy.

THE END